Stoneacre

Kent

THE NATIONAL TRUST

Perfecting Perfection

A Spanish lustreware charger on the mantelpiece in the Great Hall

Autumnal planting, including *Aster* x *frikartii* 'Mönch' and *Clematis orientalis* 'Bill MacKenzie'

(*Opposite*) The Solar

Stoneacre looks like a building that has been here for ever. Made from locally quarried limestone and the oaks that once covered the Weald of Kent, it is a perfect example of the Wealden hall-house, to which every prosperous yeoman farmer aspired in the late Middle Ages. As the name suggests, it is dominated by a central hall, in which its creator, John Ellys, would have dined communally with his servants. When he wanted greater privacy, he and his family would have retired to the smaller rooms that flank the Great Hall.

And yet all is not quite as it seems. Such houses went out of fashion in the 16th century, and as their status declined, so their fabric decayed. Stoneacre was in a sorry state by 1920, when it was rescued by the writer and antiquarian Aymer Vallance. He was a disciple of William Morris, who had revived interest in traditional English buildings like Stoneacre and shown how they could be sensitively repaired. Vallance went a step further, stripping the render off the outside of the house to reveal the half-timbering and removing other post-medieval alterations. He also added new wings that included windows and other fittings salvaged from similar ancient houses. Eighty years on, it is difficult to tell where the old house stops and the new begins. Inside, Vallance filled Stoneacre with a mixture of old sculpture, furniture, metalwork and earthenware, and modern stained glass and fabrics in the Arts and Crafts style, which had drawn inspiration from such buildings. Some are still here.

As far as possible, the National Trust has kept Stoneacre as Vallance bequeathed it in 1928, but it has encouraged the tenants to enrich the garden to make the perfect setting for this lovable house.

Aymer Vallance (1862–1943)

Aymer Vallance was a typical Oxford aesthete of the late 19th century. He combined a passion for the art and architecture of the Middle Ages with a special interest in the contemporary work of William Morris and Aubrey Beardsley; he was also an excellent cricketer.

Vallance was educated at Harrow and Oriel College, Oxford, where he read classics. In 1885 he was ordained into the Anglican Church, in 1886–8 serving as curate at the Church of the Annunciation, Brighton, which is famous for stained glass designed by Morris and Burne-Jones. However, in 1889 he was received into the Roman Catholic Church. His conversion occasioned little surprise, as Oriel College had been at the centre of the mid-19th-century Oxford Movement, which had emphasised the Catholic roots of the Church of England.

Vallance moved to London where he devoted his time to writing, lecturing on Gothic architecture, and working for the *Art Journal* and *The Studio*. He was closely associated with William Morris, publishing the first serious account of his achievements. In January 1892 he discovered the 19-year-old Aubrey Beardsley, whose drawings came as 'nothing less than a revelation'. Vallance urged him to give up working as an insurance clerk and become a full-time artist. The following month, he hosted a party to introduce Beardsley to his artistically minded friends. Morris was unimpressed, but Vallance had more luck with John Lane, publisher of *The Yellow Book*. Beardsley's work for this new

The Great Hall in 1930

4

magazine caused a sensation and made his reputation. When Beardsley was doing up his new house in Pimlico in 1893, he turned for advice to Vallance, who had written on interior decoration for the *Art Journal*. The results were startling: bright orange walls contrasted with black-painted furniture, woodwork and floors. Although Vallance disliked the increasingly decadent strain in Beardsley's work, he remained a loyal supporter, producing the first catalogue of Beardsley's drawings and preserving bookcases from the artist's Pimlico house in the library at Stoneacre.

Vallance collected medieval sculpture and woodwork, which he incorporated into the new Stoneacre or gave to the Victoria & Albert Museum. He toured the Continent, researching his articles and making a large collection of photographs, which he gave to the Courtauld Institute. His many other publications range from *Modern British Jewellery and Fans* (1902) to *Old Crosses and Lychgates* (1920) and *English Church Screens* (1939).

In 1920 at the age of 58 and still a bachelor, Vallance decided to take on Stoneacre. The following year he married Lucy Ada Hennell, who helped him to bring the house back to life.

Aymer Vallance in 1900

Vallance published these designs for playing cards in *The Yellow Book* in 1894, with Aubrey Beardsley's encouragement

One of the stained-glass panels in the Great Hall designed by Vallance

An early 16th-century Flemish or north French sculpture of St Catherine, which Vallance displayed in the Great Hall (see opposite) and bequeathed to the Victoria & Albert Museum

5

The House

Stoneacre is thought to take its name from the local limestone or Kentish rag that underlies the site and can be seen in parts of the foundations. Edward Hasted in his *History of Kent* (1778–99) records that 'John Ellys possessed this seat and resided here in the reign of King Edward II', in the early 14th century. The will of a later John Ellys of Stoneacre, who died in 1467, records the possessions of a wealthy man. In the early 1480s his son, another John Ellys, built the hall-house that forms the core of what we see today. By the middle of the 16th century the north wing (to the right of the front door) had begun to subside owing to its poor foundations and the steep slope of the ground. The present buttresses were added to stop this slippage, and the cellars, together with the ground floor, were rebuilt in stone. At the same time, an upper floor was inserted in the Great Hall to provide additional bedrooms.

In 1725 the Ellys family sold Stoneacre, and for nearly 200 years it was occupied by tenant farmers. The house gradually decayed until in 1920 it was bought, in a very dilapidated condition, by Aymer Vallance, together with ten acres.

First floor

Ground floor

STONEACRE OTHAM, KENT
1920 BEFORE RESTORATION

Restoring Stoneacre, 1920–6

The derelict state of the house gave Vallance an opportunity to use his knowledge of medieval architecture to the full. The restoration and improvements undertaken by Vallance and his architect, Marshall Harvey, were extensive. They introduced old panelling, fireplaces and windows from other ancient buildings, and added a small library and bedroom wing on the south side, for which 15th-century timber was used. They also constructed a large new north-west wing almost entirely of Tudor material from North Bore Place, a late 16th-century house which was about to be demolished at Chiddingstone in Kent. This new wing provided kitchens and domestic quarters. It is a tribute to the imagination and knowledge of Vallance that these additions do not detract from the appearance of the building. Indeed, the result is a particularly interesting restoration of a kind that was fashionable in the early 20th century, when scholarship, coupled with sensitivity, attention to detail, and ample resources, rescued some of our neglected vernacular buildings.

In 1928 Mr and Mrs Vallance gave Stoneacre to the National Trust.

First floor

Ground floor

Stoneacre during restoration: the library wing had not yet been added at the left

RESTORATION & ADDITIONS TO STONEACRE OTHAM
FOR AYMER VALLANCE ESQ

Tour of the House

The Screens Passage looks out onto the front path

The Interior
You enter the house through a massive oak front door. Vallance retrieved the original door, which had been cut down and used in another part of the house, and needed extensive restoration before it could be replaced in its correct position. The ironwork on the door is a modern reproduction, apart from the knocker, which is 16th-century and probably Flemish, and the lock, which is Elizabethan.

The Screens Passage
The Great Hall is reached through the oak screen which Vallance discovered under a

The 'Crown Post', made up of four linked columns, is a particularly rare feature of the Great Hall timberwork ceiling

layer of lath and plaster. The framework was sound, but all the panels had rotted away except for the upper one nearest the front door.

The Great Hall
The Great Hall is spanned by a gigantic tie-beam which rests on a pair of huge carved brackets; these in turn are supported by cylindrical oak shafts with polygonal moulded bases and capitals. Rising from the centre of the beam is the most remarkable feature of the Great Hall and indeed of the whole house – the Crown Post, which comprises four linked columns, a very rare pattern. The Great Hall has been carefully restored and resembles closely the character it must have had when built by John Ellys in the 1480s, though the central hearth, the smoke from which must have escaped through a louvre in the roof, was replaced with a brick and rubble chimney when the Great Hall was divided in the mid-16th century. The present chimneybreast was built in the early 1920s, incorporating a 15th-century stone fireplace from a former medieval inn, The George in Sittingbourne, and a wooden mantelpiece from a medieval cottage in Lynsted. The creatures decorating the corners of the fireplace are a fantastic kind of twin-headed snake known as an amphisbaena.

The diamond-paned glass in the two long windows of the Great Hall contains a number of quarries designed by Aymer Vallance and made by Geoffrey Webb, Horace Wilkinson and Maurice Drake. His aim was to provide just enough ornament to enliven the regular pattern of the lead beading without blocking out the light.

The six chargers over the mantelpiece are lustreware pieces made in southern Spain under Moorish influence in the late Middle Ages. Together with the oak furniture and portraits, which are mostly 17th-century, they belonged to Aymer Vallance. There are two notable coffers, one English with linenfold panelling and dated 1581, the other 16th-century Westphalian with particularly fine metalwork.

Stained glass in the Great Hall

The 16th-century chest from Westphalia in northern Germany is decorated with elaborate metal banding

The Great Hall

The Parlour

The stained glass panel of the Madonna and Child may incorporate early 15th-century work

When Vallance arrived, this was being used as the family dining room, which may always have been its function. He introduced the 16th-century fireplace, which came from North Bore Place. The stained glass in the north window features a Madonna and Child, the main part of which is thought to be early 15th-century. The other quarries are reproductions of late Gothic glass, some designed by Vallance and executed by Wilfred Drake. The curtains are a rare survival: the pattern is *The Angel with the Trumpet*, designed by Herbert Horne around 1884 for the Century Guild. The Century Guild was formed in 1882 by Arthur Haygate Mackmurdo 'to render all branches of art the sphere no longer of the tradesman but of the artist. It would restore building decoration, glass painting, pottery, wood carving and metal to their right place beside painting and sculpture.' The aims of the Century Guild were close to Vallance's heart.

The plates on the mantelpiece and the wall are 19th-century Chinese. The portraits are of Mr and Mrs William Vallance, Aymer Vallance's grandparents, and of James Orwood Vallance (dated 14 June 1857), his uncle. The architectural drawings show the extensive alterations made between 1920 and 1926. The furniture is oak, mostly 17th-century, except for the bobbin chairs with the leather seats, which are turned elm.

The *Angel with the Trumpet* hanging in the Parlour was designed by the Arts and Crafts artist and writer Herbert Horne around 1884. Horne later gave his collection of Italian Renaissance art to the city of Florence

(*Opposite*) The Parlour

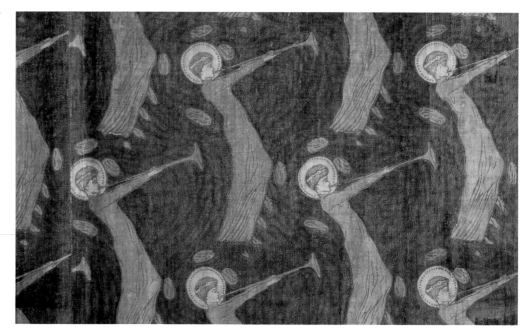

The door to the Solar has exceptionally elaborate hinges

Vallance furnished the Solar with mainly 17th-century oak pieces

(*Right*) This abstract window on the staircase has an Art Nouveau flavour

(*Opposite*) The spiral staircase was added by Vallance

The Lobby

The Lobby, which links the old and new parts of the house, is furnished with 17th-century oak furniture and 17th- and 18th-century portraits.

The Staircase

The Staircase came from North Bore Place and is made from solid blocks of oak, which have had the angle removed from the underside to create a continuous spiral like a screw. Vallance designed a number of the stained-glass quarries.

The Solar

In medieval times, the Solar was usually the principal upstairs living room, but such rooms were often used as bedrooms. The ceiling is similar to that in the Great Hall, but on a smaller scale and without capitals on the cluster-column crown base. The fireplace is original, and the oriel window, although entirely conjectural in detail, follows the plan of the original. Some of the quarries were designed by Vallance. The grooves that run from floor to ceiling on either side of the two flanking windows were made to carry vertical sliding shutters, a very uncommon detail. The furniture is mostly 17th-century English oak, with the exception of the 17th-century walnut table with carved frieze and the 17th-century Flemish oak hanging cupboard with carved panels in the upper parts of its doors. The portraits are 17th-century.

The Garden

An *acuminata* tulip

The garden at Stoneacre has evolved over the centuries, but still retains its old-world character, in keeping with the ancient house. During the last two decades the tenants have done much to enrich the planting within the existing framework.

The entrance to the garden is dominated by a rare tree, *Ginkgo biloba*. The stone path leading to the house is edged with *Alchemilla mollis* (Lady's Mantle) and *Muscari* grape hyacinths. In 2001 a small rose garden was planted, hidden behind a yew hedge. The roses are all old varieties and the colours range from red and deep purple to pink. The green, gold and brown borders around the lawns on either side of the front path remain of interest throughout the year, seasonal changes being achieved with annuals and bulbs.

Through a small arch in the dividing garden wall there is a dark border containing many plants with dark flowers or leaves, including a fine display of 'Queen of Night' and 'Black Swan' tulips in the spring and an unusual black-leaved *Anthriscus sylvestris* 'Ravenswing'. A large *Staphylea colchica* shades the east end of this part of the garden. The lawn is framed by a red border and a purple border. Early in the season, these borders have a more delicate appearance, while in high summer there is additional planting to give a bright display of cannas and dahlias. Steps and paths on a higher level offer good views of the garden. From the small courtyard at the rear of the house a grass bank leads to a summer-house, giving views over the apple orchards. Grass paths are cut through the meadows of wild flowers.

The opening in the old stone wall in the front garden leads to a border featuring plants with dark flowers and leaves

(Opposite) The old stone path to the front door is edged with grape hyacinths (*Muscari armenicum*) in spring